For Joyce Allwright

With kind regards
Richard Gaunt
Feb. 2013

Emma's Sketchbook

Scenes of Nottinghamshire Life in the 1840s

edited by Richard A Gaunt

In memory of Neville Hoskins – who rescued Emma from obscurity

ABOUT THE AUTHOR

Dr Richard A Gaunt is Associate Professor in Modern British History at the University of Nottingham and a Fellow of the Royal Historical Society. He has edited the diaries of the 4th Duke of Newcastle in two volumes (2003, 2006) and written widely on electoral politics in Nottinghamshire in the early nineteenth century. Dr Gaunt was managing editor of *Transactions of the Thoroton Society of Nottinghamshire* (2008-2010) and his *Politics, Law and Society in Nottinghamshire, The Diaries of Godfrey Tallents of Newark, 1829-1839* was published by Nottinghamshire County Council in 2010.

ISBN: 978-0-902751-74-3

Designed and printed by:
Nottinghamshire County Council,
Design and Print, 2013.

CONTENTS

EMMA AND WILMOT - THEIR LIVES AND WORLD

On 30 December 1841, Edward Woollett Wilmot wrote to his employer, the 4th Duke of Newcastle-under-Lyne, at Clumber Park in Nottinghamshire, requesting leave of absence for a most important occasion:

> On the 13th of next month, my marriage is to take place, if
> Your Grace can kindly give me about ten days...I purpose
> [*sic*] going to see my father at Brighton immediately after the
> day - I can make all due arrangements here, that nothing shall
> stand still during my absence - I shall call here in the morning
> on my way to Nottingham - and shall be here again on
> Tuesday [1].

Wilmot's bride was Emma Elizabeth Darwin. The marriage duly took place on 13 January 1842 at St Helen's Church in Darley Dale, near Bakewell, Derbyshire. It was the start of a union which would last over twenty two years and lead the couple to reside, successively, in Nottinghamshire, Cheshire and Derbyshire, in furtherance of Wilmot's career as a land agent and surveyor of some importance.

Like many individuals of her gender and station, Emma Wilmot left relatively little trace in the written record of her age. However, unlike most of them, she was an artist of no mean distinction whose charming and evocative drawings of Nottinghamshire life in the first five years of her marriage (1842-1847) reveal a lively eye and technical skill in capturing the picturesque details of her day. Whilst the larger part of her life can only be glimpsed through the better-recorded history of her husband, some understanding of that life and the largely rural context within which it was located not only helps to explain the pre-occupation with architecture and the natural world which Emma Wilmot's drawings reveal but also tells us something about the character of the artist herself.

[Left: St Helen's Church, Darley Dale]

Emma and Wilmot

Both Emma and Wilmot came from well-established, well-connected country families. Emma Elizabeth Darwin was born on 27 February 1820 at Lichfield in Staffordshire [see **Emma's drawing bottom right**]; she was baptised at St Mary's Church, in the town, on 24 March. Emma was the third of

the ten children (and second eldest daughter) of Francis Sacheverel Darwin (17 June 1786-6 November 1859), physician, and Jane Harriett Ryle (1794-1866). Francis was one of the six surviving children of Erasmus Darwin (1731-1802), the Nottinghamshire-born physician, poet and naturalist, who played a leading part in the eighteenth century English enlightenment, by his marriage to Elizabeth Pole of Derby. Emma was thus a first-cousin of Charles Darwin, her senior by eleven years, whose theories of natural selection caused so much controversy after the publication of *On the Origin of Species* in 1859. Given the intellectual pedigree of the Darwin family over successive generations, it is clear that Emma was raised as part of a lively, enquiring household in which archaeology and natural history were the principal topics of conversation. Emma's father, who (in his youth)

had travelled extensively through Spain, the Mediterranean and the East, was knighted by George IV in the year of her birth and served as a deputy Lord Lieutenant of Derbyshire. He was devoted to the county; though he had a medical practice for a short period in Lichfield, in emulation of his father Erasmus (who had been resident in the cathedral close from 1758-81), Francis Darwin spent the larger part of his life in the family home at Breadsall Priory near Derby: after his death, a plaque was erected to his memory in Breadsall All Saints' Church.

Edward Woollett Wilmot was equally well-connected to the Derbyshire gentry. His father was Sir Robert Wilmot (3rd baronet) of Chaddesden (5 July 1765-13 July 1842) and his mother Lucy Grimston (20 August 1772-May 1812). Wilmot, who was baptised at Chaddesden on 3 August 1808, had five older brothers. The second eldest, Henry Sacheverel Wilmot, the future 4th baronet (baptised on 11 February 1801, died 11 April 1872), married Maria Mundy, of the Mundy family of Shipley Hall, at St Lawrence's Church, Heanor, Derbyshire, on 13 December 1826. This created a

residual family connection between Wilmot and his future employer, the 4th Duke of Newcastle, who was married to Georgiana Miller Mundy, of the same family, between 1807 and 1822.

Emma Darwin was Wilmot's second wife. On 3 February 1831, Edward married, at Uppingham in Rutland, Augusta Matilda Champion (born c.1809), the daughter of Charles Champion esquire of Beaumont Chase, Plymouth. The marriage produced a number of  children: Lucy Augusta (baptised 8 January 1832), Edward Woollett (baptised 25 November 1832, died 13 April 1833), Robert Charles (baptised 11 January 1834) and Edward – universally known as Edmund - (baptised 12 June 1836). At this period, the family were living at Pickwell, on the border between Leicestershire and Rutland. It was conveniently located not only for Leicester (sixteen miles away) but for the major agricultural centres of Melton Mowbray and Oakham (six miles distant). In keeping with his status as an 'esquire' and 'gentleman', Wilmot was a member of the Leicestershire yeomanry cavalry [2].

[Left: Emma's drawing of Chaddesden Hall, Wilmot's family home]

Of the children produced by Wilmot's first marriage, the eldest surviving son (Robert Charles) married Elizabeth (born 1838), daughter of William Henry Robertson, at St John's Church, Buxton, on 11 April 1861. His second son, Edmund, who was described in his obituary as a 'strong Churchman, and a staunch Conservative', was appointed keeper of the Judge's Lodgings in St Mary's Gate, Derby in 1886. After suffering from gout and other internal complaints for many years, he died on 24 November 1896 and was buried at Kirk Langley in Derbyshire three days later [3]. Wilmot's eldest daughter (Lucy Augusta), married - at Astbury, Cheshire, on 5 April 1853 - Christopher Percy Soulsby of Bessingby, Yorkshire (baptised 13 July 1828, died in New Zealand January 1867), a land agent who had served his apprenticeship in Wilmot's household. Following Lucy's death, on 10 March 1854, Soulsby went on to marry (the following year) Susan Sybilla Thompson (19 November 1833-9 February 1904), the daughter of Jonathan Thompson of Wellow Hall, Nottinghamshire. Soulsby named his son Ralph Wilmot and his daughter Lucy Helen Muriel (1856-1927) in remembrance of his first wife [4].

By the mid-1830s, Wilmot was a married man with three young children gaining a high reputation as an agriculturist for his expertise in rearing valuable breeding stock, including sheep, cows, pigs and horses. His animal husbandry at Pickwell marked him out amongst contemporaries for his 'spirit' and for the 'unusual success' which attended him when exhibiting livestock at agricultural shows in Leicestershire, Rutland, Lincolnshire and Northamptonshire [5]. Wilmot also served as President of the Derbyshire Agricultural Society, judged at the North Derbyshire Agricultural Society and was a steward at the annual Smithfield Cattle Club show. By 1840, Wilmot was a governor of the English Agricultural Society and on the committee of the newly-formed Farmer's Fire and Life Institution [6]. Wilmot also established his credentials as a land agent and steward to the great landowners in the area. Through his connection to the Saviles of Rufford (Earls of Scarbrough), Wilmot came into occupation of Wellow Farm, near Ollerton in Nottinghamshire, in 1837 [7].

Agent to the Duke (1838-1848)

It was through his connection with Scarbrough that Wilmot first became acquainted with the 4th Duke of Newcastle. When the Duke's land agent and steward (John Parkinson) left Clumber in the autumn of 1838, it was to Wilmot that Newcastle turned: 'I believe I have made a good choice in appointing Mr Edward Wilmot who I believe & hope is well qualified for the undertakings - I have today made the final arrangements & I give Mr Wilmot £800 a year. He is to devote himself to my business alone & engage in nothing else' [8]. The Duke's determination to have an agent solely occupied with his own business was characteristic of his dealings with stewards and would lead to

turbulent relations between the two men in succeeding years; in December 1838, Wilmot was still undertaking Scarbrough's rent audits [9]. However, at the commencement of Wilmot's appointment, Newcastle was more than satisfied with his new employee, commenting that Wilmot had 'remitted a larger sum by nearly double that [sic] has heretofore been paid to my account by my former Steward'. The Duke had it on his own and others' account that Wilmot was a man of 'good feeling & high notions', a situation which he had 'reason to hope he will steadily & inflexibly maintain' [10].

At the time of his appointment to the Newcastle agency, Wilmot was still married to Augusta Champion and still corresponding from Pickwell, but the next few years affected material changes in his personal situation. After the sale of the livestock at Pickwell, in October 1839, Wilmot came into possession of 'Sparken' (afterwards known as Sparken House), one of the few substantial properties to be found on Sparken Hill, Worksop before the late-nineteenth century. The area (which regularly appeared in contemporary accounts as 'Sparkin') had been planted from 1762. It passed into Newcastle's ownership, following his purchase of the Worksop Manor estate from the 12th Duke of Norfolk, in 1838-9. Sparken provided Wilmot's family with their Nottinghamshire home for the next decade and featured in a number of Emma's drawings [see right].

Whilst Sparken House was demolished in the mid- to late-1950s, as part of the re-development of the site for a new school, the farm (which Wilmot rented at £200 per annum) is still extant; together with a two-storey detached building, there are boiler houses, barns and greenhouses, a substantial brick with pan tile roof barn, ground floor stabling and tack-room [11].

Wilmot's first wife, Augusta, died on 21 December 1838, within months of their move to Worksop. Wilmot placed a memorial tablet to his 'beloved wife' on the wall facing the south porch of Worksop Priory Church; the text came from Luke 8:52 'she died but she only sleepeth'. The cause of her death is still unknown. Wilmot mentioned his wife's illness in a letter to Newcastle at the time, but without detailing the particulars [12]. Wilmot's letters to the Duke are only partially self-revealing, insofar as his family are concerned, and he was usually led into such revelations from a determination to defend himself against the Duke's repeated charges of neglect of estate business. For example, in 1839, Wilmot referred to a birth defect affecting the roof of his daughter's mouth and a discharge from his son's ears, which necessitated his consulting London doctors. Several years later, there is reference to his eldest daughter being very ill and an acknowledgement of Newcastle's assistance on behalf of Wilmot's son, during his father's absence from the county [13]. Nevertheless, though there is little to indicate how or when Emma Darwin came into Wilmot's life, a reasonable surmise can be made that, as the product of two well-connected country families, they are likely to have enjoyed shared company in Derbyshire society on numerous occasions and that, out of this, developed the relationship which ultimately led to their marriage.

Married Life at Sparken (1842-1847)

Emma and Wilmot had four children during their time at Sparken Hill. These were Emma Maria (c.1843-26 June 1927), Frances Jane – or Fanny – (c.1844-26 January 1929), Darwin (14 October 1845-5 September 1935) and Woollett (born 10 April 1847). The dictates of a growing family were ever-present in Wilmot's mind, throughout the 1840s, as political uncertainty over the future economic protection of agriculture reared its head as a prominent public issue. As Wilmot informed Newcastle, in February 1846, when the threat of unemployment beckoned, with a wife and six children to support, he needed employment, for 'as an idle man I must starve - my income depends upon my work'. The same impulse led him, as agent, to arrange for an increase in labourers' wages, on the grounds that, 'with flour at 4 shillings 10 pence per stone and no potatoes – a man with 5 or 6 children will consume very nearly 4 stone per week – he has therefore but little for meat, house, rent or clothes' [14]. Wilmot also remained solicitous on behalf of his wider family – in 1844, he requested two days leave of absence from the Duke in order to assist his brother, who was letting his house at Brighton. Three years later, he requested first refusal on a farm and house formerly occupied by Miss Cousins at North Muskham, on behalf of his brother [15]. Wilmot was no less forthcoming with Emma's relatives. When Reverend Webster resigned his Anglican living at Worksop, in 1845, Wilmot advanced the claims of his brother-in-law, Mr Barton:

> living at Congleton in Cheshire with a parish of 4000 and an income of £150... he is certainly not a low Churchman, nor on the other hand is he a Puseyite...I have always heard him most highly spoken of - the only point I can speak confidently upon, is, his, having a wife in every way calculated for a parish clergyman - she being a daughter of Sir F Darwin's - his own qualifications must rest upon the character he has established [16].

Differences with the Duke

Despite the auspicious start to the two men's relationship, communications between Wilmot and Newcastle soon began to adopt a tone of defensiveness on the one part and criticism on the other which was to drive them apart as the decade progressed. As early as November 1839, Wilmot observed that he was 'much obliged' to Newcastle for 'kindly pointing out where you think I have failed' [17]. At this period, the issue seems to have been Newcastle's sense that, during his absences in London and Wales, he was not being kept informed of developments at Clumber. Newcastle was also determined to be consulted about estate matters which required his sanction and expense. 'I always feel afraid of intruding too much', Wilmot responded, 'unless there is something of moment to communicate...I have not during your absence, commenced or done anything, of which Your Grace was not fully aware, and have endeavoured to the best in my power to curtail every expence [sic]'. Within a few years, however, the Duke's criticism had extended to more material facts – including Wilmot's method of keeping accounts and the authorisation of maintenance work and repairs (including drainage and building) [18].

Increasingly, Newcastle seems to have felt that Wilmot was not prosecuting the recovery of arrears from tenants or the sale of property with sufficient energy. On both counts, Wilmot's sense of wounded pride was evident in his responses: 'I will do everything in my power to urge the payment [of arrears]', he commented in 1844, 'it is most disheartening – and causes me more annoyance than I can express – it is certainly not for want of severity upon my part, for I did not spare them'. As to the sale of property, Wilmot pointed out – 'you will I hope clearly understand my object is to make the best I can of the property – a good sale must redound to my credit, a bad one, necessarily to the reverse – therefore, unless I am an arrant rogue, my only motive can be to secure a prosperous issue'. Unfortunately, as time progressed, Newcastle came to think that Wilmot was 'little better than a rascal' [19].

Newcastle clearly had history when it came to abusing his agents for neglect of business. In 1839, Wilmot's predecessor, John Parkinson, had expressed the somewhat rueful hope that Wilmot would 'hold his situation for a much longer period than I had the honour to do, and with greater satisfaction to Your Grace, and with that almost invariable deference and respect I experienced from your numerous tenantry' – but Parkinson had been the Duke's steward since 1822 and had clearly learned how to manage relations with him over the long-term [20]. Wilmot, by contrast, raised Newcastle's ire by accepting commissions for work from other people. For example, in 1844, Wilmot undertook the valuation of properties at Cold Overton and Knossington in Leicestershire on behalf of Thomas Frewen of Brickwall House, Northiam, near Rye in Sussex [21].

Wilmot's perceived encouragement of the railway mania of the 1840s, by which speculators drove lines adjacent to (or through) existing landed estates, also provoked Newcastle's opposition. Wilmot's growing reputation as an agent and surveyor led him to be called in aid by a number of railway companies and he was summoned as a witness before parliamentary committees on individual schemes. For example, in 1845, Wilmot gave evidence which attempted to prove injury to the Gedling estate on the grounds that the proposed line spoiled the view from the lodge and destroyed the preserves [22].

However, at the end of 1845, Wilmot's name appeared as one of the provisional directors of the Ambergate, Nottingham and Boston and Eastern Junction Railway, which raised Newcastle's suspicions of a conflict of interests on his agent's part [23]. Two years later, Wilmot defended his conduct in the intervening period: 'I never was employed by the Sheffield and Lincolnshire [Railway Company], excepting to give Evidence [to Parliament] in 1845 – in 1846 they wished me again to do so but I declined… as you were opposing their Bill – on the Canal Line as it was called – I last year, valued some portions of their line avoiding Your Grace's property'. Remarking of the increased business he was likely to gain by continuing to advance Newcastle's opposition even where the prospects looked grim, Wilmot remarked: 'looking to my own selfish interest, I ought to encourage the opposition – but looking to your's I think very differently' [24].

As was so often the case with Newcastle, who was a noted ultra-Tory, it was political differences which finally drove the two men apart. Initially, Wilmot's knowledge and connections had proved politically useful to the Duke. In advance of the General Election of 1841, Newcastle noted with pride that Wilmot had 'been doing all he can to forward the elections hereabouts to a favourable termination'. He had also used his connections at Derby to sound out a possible candidacy by the Duke's younger son, Lord William Pelham-Clinton [25]. The real difficulty arose four years later. After news of an emerging potato famine in Ireland reached England, and in the face of the persistent campaigning of the Anti-Corn Law League, the Conservative government of Sir Robert Peel, which had been elected in 1841 on a platform of agricultural protection and defence of the corn laws, announced their gradual relaxation and repeal. The Earl of Lincoln, Newcastle's son and heir and a close political and personal friend of Peel, decided to support this measure wholeheartedly. When Lincoln proceeded to accept a government office which necessitated standing for re-election in South Nottinghamshire, all manner of local interests were upset. The ensuing by-election contest turned upon a combination of personalities (Lincoln being a well respected and popular MP), issues (considering the importance of agriculture within Nottinghamshire) and influence (given the political and economic interests of the great county landowners and the political sentiments of the tenant farmers themselves) **[26]**.

Wilmot was awkwardly placed in all of this. As a near-contemporary of Lincoln, the two men were close personally but Wilmot had spoken strongly in defence of the corn laws at a protectionist meeting at Derby in 1844 and was the public face of Newcastle's interests in the county. Newcastle would brook no talk of corn law repeal and went so far as to intervene personally against Lincoln in the ensuing election contest. Throughout this period, Wilmot maintained a correspondence with Lincoln on the subject, offering him detailed political and electoral advice and making his personal support for him abundantly clear:

the course you have laid down seems the only manly open one - as

to apologies I would never descend to them - you were returned to do your best for the country, and if you do that however your views may differ from other persons, that best you have done, and more cannot be done by any one - the farmers are generally bigotted [sic] and narrow-minded - they would stand by and see their neighbours starving, with unconcern, but breathe a word as to their pockets and they are frantic...your succession from the county would not only punish them, but would be a serious loss to those good & true men who were alike convinced of your rectitude of heart and purpose **[27]**.

Having volunteered his assistance to Lincoln – 'I will not fail to apprise you of any new steps in the county, and will do my best to find out the views of all I can' **[28]** – Wilmot proceeded to attend a meeting of the Nottinghamshire Agricultural Protection Society which drew down upon him the unqualified vitriol of the Duke. 'Wilmot caught it the next morning in a letter of much violence [the Duke's election agent, Godfrey Tallents, told Lincoln] charging him with being a Peelite and a Leaguer – However as Wilmot moved a resolution against the League and spoke with good affect [sic] your father's impression may go off'. Wilmot, never one to take Newcastle's criticisms lying-down, responded that he had 'fully approved' the government's measures of 'Income tax, the Tariff, & the Poor Law Bills...and was determined to support them to my best in every way - & that I had full hope the measures to be proposed [now] would be found just & honest – if they were not so I should be ready to join him in opposing them, but not otherwise' [29].

Newcastle's revenge was to suggest an alteration in Wilmot's remit as agent which would deprive him of responsibility for the Nottingham Collection and leave him with oversight of the Clumber Collection [30]. 'With regard to the Nottingham Collection [Wilmot responded], I took it gratuitously because I believed I could not only save you the salary of a person there, but also considerably increase the rental of the property – these I have done – more might...still be accomplished, by a person residing near, and giving more attention than I could do at this distance'. Wilmot had no option but to apply for the position, citing family reasons as a strong inducement why he would prefer the position to remaining at Worksop:

> I should be in the neighbourhood of my own connections, and in
> every way better situated than I am here - both as to my own comfort,
> and the education of my children - I should also be near enough to
> Clumber to give any assistance to Your Grace, which it would not
> only be my duty but a great pride to me to do, whenever
> opportunities required - my proposal would be, that the arrangement
> should commence next November, when my eighth year will be
> completed at Clumber - the rental will be then cleared of arrears,
> whatever new tenants are required will be settled in their farms,
> and I flatter myself, all things in a fair and straight form [31].

When Newcastle responded with a further charge of perceived neglect, Wilmot renewed his wish to have first refusal on the Nottingham Collection and regretted 'the painful conviction that...I have by some means lost that confidence, without which I am well convinced I cannot be useful to you – to state this gives me more pain than I can express'. Given this state of affairs, Wilmot decided against appearing at Lincoln's nomination for South Nottinghamshire, calculating that as he was 'still the Duke's agent, and his views being now well known, my appearance in public might only tend to irritate His Grace and your opponents, and give grounds for the now generally believed falsehood, that I have canvassed his tenants in your favour' [32].

Wilmot's discretion in not publicly exposing his political differences with Newcastle, by attending the election hustings, did not affect a rapprochement with the Duke. Still uncertain as to his future prospects, Wilmot began canvassing for other employment, soliciting a vacant post at the Duchy of Lancaster and seeking a new farmer for Sparken, where his tenant (Stuart) was about to leave: 'the farm is too important to be carelessly tenanted', he told Lincoln [33]. Though Lincoln lost his election for South Nottinghamshire, Newcastle made clear his lasting displeasure with Wilmot's support for him when, in May, 'he alluded to my retiring, but would enter into no explanation – I asked him as to the Nottingham Collection, he said he had better part altogether, and that he proposed remodelling every thing [sic] – I therefore quit in November, and commence the world again on my own account'. When Wilmot's successor later declined taking the Nottingham Collection as part of his role, Wilmot renewed his entreaties for the position, informing Newcastle that 'being engaged to look over the estates of as strong a protectionist as yourself near Nottingham would be a sufficient guarantee that I should not interfere against the views of those for whom I was engaged'. However, it was too late to expect a reprieve from Newcastle and, for Wilmot, the future looked anything but encouraging: 'I cannot help feeling anxious upon the result [he told Lincoln], as six children are a heavy charge - however as I am ready and willing to work, and have some little experience I hope for the best - should you ever have an opportunity of naming me to any of your friends I shall feel greatly obliged' [34].

Newcastle did not find it easy to find a successor to Wilmot, but the certain knowledge that such a successor would (in due course) be forthcoming, necessitated that Wilmot start diversifying his interests. By 1848, Wilmot had begun acting as agent to Robert Holden of Nuthall Temple, Nottinghamshire, in succession to George Hodgkinson, who had fulfilled the role since 1826 [35]. Throughout 1848 and 1849, Wilmot was also kept busy producing maps on behalf of the Tithe Commissioners. Surveys bearing Wilmot's imprint survive for a range of parishes across Derbyshire and Cheshire, including Calow near Chesterfield, Denby near Derby and Marton, Siddington and Capesthorne near Prestbury. Wilmot also acted as an Enclosure Commissioner for Newbold in Warwickshire and Dalbury near Derby

[36]. However, Newcastle continued to regard Wilmot as solely at his bidding until his successor was in place: 'Your Grace is quite wrong in supposing I am neglecting your work', Wilmot complained in June 1847, 'I have it is true taken six agencies since January but all I have obtained unsolicited – and made the same stipulation with each that I could not attend to them properly until I left your appointment – I have also other work to attend to, which I am obliged to neglect at great loss to myself' [37].

In due course, Henry Heming (who would act as agent to the Newcastle estates during the remainder of the 4th Duke's lifetime and for nearly all of Lincoln's time as 5th Duke of Newcastle), was fixed upon as a suitable successor. He came with the recommendation of his former employer (and Newcastle's fellow ultra-Tory), Lord Falmouth, but with the additional complication - from the Duke's perspective - of being known and liked by Wilmot himself [38]. 'Mr Heming is a very good man, and one who I think you will approve of [Wilmot told the Duke] he will at all times find me most willing to afford any information in my power'. When Heming proceeded to stay at Sparken during a preliminary visit to the county, in the summer of 1847, Newcastle made his displeasure clear. Matters were complicated when Heming told Wilmot that it was commonly reported that, upon Lincoln's succeeding to the title, Wilmot was to be reinstated as agent. 'I have felt so much annoyed at the idea [Wilmot told the Duke in denying the assertion] that I cannot refrain from naming it to Your

Grace...and I hope you would do me the justice not to believe any such report' **[39]**. Heming was also full of contrition: 'I had no idea that you would disapprove of my accepting Mr Wilmot's invitation to remain at his house...Having known Mr Wilmot before, & my business being with him, I did not think there was any impropriety'. As to the rumours, they were 'of common report – I heard it from various quarters, and did not, therefore, regard it as a secret...I trust Your Grace will allow me to claim from you what I think is justly due to me that you will never form an unfavourable judgment upon the report of any words or actions of mine by another until you have allowed me the opportunity of denial or explanation' **[40]**.

Relations between Wilmot and Heming had now been soured by their determination to remain unsullied by any accusations of impropriety levelled against them and by an awareness of the Duke's hyper-sensitivity on the subject of loyalty. Having made all his arrangements for quitting Sparken in time for Heming's scheduled arrival on 1 August 1847, Wilmot subsequently charged his successor with bad faith in postponing 'until the 11th 17th & 19th and on the 24th he is not arrived – and not only is it inconvenient but it makes me appear as neglecting your affairs...I do not however name this with any idea of blaming Your Grace, because you must be if anything more inconvenienced than I am' **[41]**. Newcastle was, himself, inconvenienced – less by constant changes of schedule than the perception that, in exchanging Wilmot with Heming, his difficulties

were not necessarily over:

> [Mr Heming] is one of the hardest & closest bargainers I ever met with. Money seems to be his great object – but I must hope that he will take as good care of my money as of his own – he is to have a salary of £800 – to cover everything – to take & engage in no other business besides mine – to live in Wilmot's present house & to take his farm but at a reduced rent of £160 – instead of 200 - & to give a bond of security of £12,000 **[42]**.

There followed a rather messy closing of accounts between Newcastle and Wilmot. As early as November 1847, Wilmot was trying to explain to Newcastle that the uncertainty surrounding Heming had complicated his financial affairs: 'there are several items relating to my late residence [Sparken] unsettled which I do not know whether they are to be charged to Your Grace or to Mr Heming...there is a balance due to me on the accounts exclusive of my salary to the time of my quitting'. Wilmot closed his accounts with Smith & Company, Bankers of Nottingham, at the end of 1848 but a further two months elapsed before Newcastle requested a final settlement of accounts between the two men **[43]**. However, a rough and unsigned abstract which Wilmot had prepared for the purpose was forwarded to the Duke in error, resulting in an angry epistle from the latter fulminating 'that any man who laid claim to respectability or punctuality in business could have ventured so to peril his reputation as to send such an account & so to conduct himself towards his employer…in short the account is as disgraceful as it is utterly unsatisfactory'. After threatening Wilmot with all manner of legal sanctions and threats to 'caution your present employers as to the danger of there [*sic*] situation' [44], Wilmot responded with a rational defence of the charges laid to his account in respect of Sparken:

> prior to my leaving Worksop, I urged Your Grace, to appoint some one to go into my claims, stating I only wanted a fair and honest valuation, this I again repeat, I have told Mr Heming time after time if I have charged any thing I am not legally entitled to, I am ready at once to take it out of the account - I could never get any answer - and I was compelled to have my property valued before leaving [45].

The matter thus embroiled Heming, who was forced to assure Newcastle 'that I have not intentionally done a single act to aid or defend Mr Wilmot in his accounts, nor am I responsible for the entries made to his credit'. In self-defence, Heming alluded to the difficulty of inheriting an accounting system with which he was unfamiliar: 'Any person accustomed to Your Grace's system of accounts could understand this: but a stranger to them might be perplexed – To the form of account Your Grace has obliged me to adhere therefore I cannot be responsible for any defects in the system'. This was the self-same system of accounting which Newcastle had insisted upon being adopted by Wilmot several years earlier [46].

After Sparken (1848-1864)

Though they continued to retain business and social connections with the county, Wilmot, Emma and their family had left Nottinghamshire by the end of the decade. After quitting Sparken, in the autumn of 1847 (leaving behind 'the greater part' of their furniture), the family moved to Etwall Lodge near Derby, where (as Wilmot informed Lincoln), he was 'near the railway and [could] reach any point at a small cost and in a short time' [47]. From 1848, Wilmot began advertising his address as Hulme Walfield, a small township four miles from Astbury and two miles from Congleton in Cheshire. The family settled at Daisy Bank, overlooking the River Dane valley [48]. In the 1851 Census, in addition to Wilmot, Emma and five children (Lucy, Emma Maria, Frances Jane, Darwin and Woollett), the household contained Christopher Soulsby (afterwards Wilmot's son-in-law), three land agent pupils, a governess and seven servants. During their time in Cheshire, Emma gave birth to a further son, Reginald Mead Wilmot (baptised 12 June 1852-17 December 1920) [49].

Wilmot's move to Hulme Walfield arose from his appointment, in 1848, as steward to the Capesthorne estates of Arthur Henry Davenport (9 June 1832-7 September 1867). However, much as previously, Wilmot combined this role with other commissions. For example, in 1850, he produced a report on 5000 acres of land which were proposed to become part of the estate of Charles Broderick,

Viscount Midleton [*sic*], in County Cork and County Waterford, Ireland. The report, containing a range of recommendations relating to letting agreements and tenancies, railways, land improvement and drainage, is indicative of Wilmot's thinking as an agent and his desire to effect lasting improvements, under the right conditions. For example, Wilmot recommended doing away with leases 'as opportunities offer' and adopting an agreement that would compensate tenants for 'unexhausted improvements' (the report included a sample letting agreement and architectural sketch plans for farm yards, farm houses and out-buildings). Given his close interest in railways, it is unsurprising to find Wilmot recommending the introduction of railways, the widening of rivers and the drainage of swamps. Throughout, Wilmot expressed the desire to encourage 'enterprising and industrious' tenants who could make material, lasting changes to the landscape. Wilmot's authority on the subject of tenancy agreements led him to be called as a witness before a parliamentary select committee on agricultural customs in March 1848; his methods were also quoted with approval by contemporary authorities on the subject [50].

The growing demand for Wilmot's services as a land agent and continuing work as a livestock judge (for example, at the Liverpool and Manchester agricultural show) kept him well-occupied during his residence in Cheshire; by the 1850s, he was advertising his offices jointly at Hulme Walfield and Broughton Grange (Park Lane, Broughton) near Manchester [51]. However, the high-point of Wilmot's career – and the position which came closest to his and Emma's Derbyshire roots – was his appointment, in August 1856, in succession to Sydney Smithers, as agent for the 6th Duke of Devonshire's Buxton estate. The appointment arose from Smithers' death and was continued after the 7th Duke succeeded to his estates and title in 1858. Wilmot's departure from Hulme Walfield, after nine years as steward of the Capesthorne estates, was marked by a dinner attended by the tenant farmers of the district at which he was presented with a silver kettle 'of elaborate manufacture, and of the most chaste design', featuring his family crest on one side. In returning thanks, Wilmot acknowledged that he was accepting employment from Devonshire 'not to please you, but to better myself' and hoped that he could be inspired by their example 'to do more' [52].

Buxton was a settlement of some 1800 people in 1856 and its development as a spa town had already begun during the lengthy agencies of Philip Heathcote (1801-51) and Smithers (1851-6). However, 'it required a man of vision...courage, perseverance and industry to press forward the measures which would lay the foundation for [it to become] a progressive town and watering place'. Buxton lacked both self-government and the railways together with many of the urban amenities which would attract regular visitors and a flourishing retail and manufacturing workforce. Wilmot's vision for the improvement and development of Buxton, through changes to its infrastructure, drainage, gas and water supply, leisure amenities and educational facilities, were outlined in an important public lecture on 'Town Improvements', which he delivered at the Buxton and Fairfield Mechanics Institute in December 1859. This became the blue-print for subsequent developments over the next five years.

Wilmot's position as ducal agent (as well as his long-standing interests) led him to become President of the local Agricultural and Horticultural Clubs and President of the Buxton and Burbage Building Societies. Wilmot was instrumental in the development of the Market Hall and, even more importantly, the adoption of the Local Government Act in the town which gave it important powers of self-regulation. All of this accorded with the sentiments contained in his Midleton Estate Report and 'Town Improvements' lecture. As first Chairman of the Local Board for Fairfield and Buxton, from June 1859, Wilmot influenced the growth of the town through the provision of new streets, ornamental gardens, footpaths, a cattle market (September 1861) and new fire-fighting, water and sewerage systems. With the influx of railway workers to the town, a reading room was provided for the use of navvies (June 1861). Wilmot was also instrumental in changes to the Buxton Endowed School, of which he became a trustee and treasurer, with resident trustees appointed after March 1862 and provision made for the education of all children between four and sixteen in Latin, English and Writing. The railways finally came to Buxton in May and June 1863, Wilmot having used his considerable expertise as a land agent and surveyor to charge the Midland and London North West companies £400 per acre for building land and £100 an acre for farm land. However, the most significant of Wilmot's achievements was in persuading the Duke of Devonshire to convert the former Cavendish stables into the Devonshire hospital, in order to admit patients who had applied to the Buxton Bath Charity. In the face of notable opposition from, amongst others, Joseph Paxton, the Duke was persuaded to allow the conversion of the site with provision for between 100 and 150 beds. Wilmot was treasurer of the New Hospital Charity, which was opened to patients in January 1859 [53].

Wilmot's desire for change and impatience with local resistance became increasingly apparent as the years passed. He failed to persuade the Local Board to accept an offer by the directors of the Gas Company to sell out to them – a decision he imputed to 'incompetence, jealousy and spite among the local officials, which he did not understand'. More seriously, during 1863, Wilmot was criticised for engaging Robert Rawlinson to design a sewerage system for the town which would be connected to (and paid for by) all the properties. The Board rejected the proposal and were supported by the Secretary of State who deemed it unlawful for all properties to be connected to the system in this way. After Devonshire talked the issue over with Wilmot, in November 1863, both men agreed that the best course of action was for Wilmot to resign as Chairman. Privately, Devonshire thought that Wilmot had 'not been altogether judicious' in his proceedings and was 'inclined to think that his presence on the board is really rather injurious to his influence than otherwise' [54].

However, the good feeling which generally subsisted between Wilmot and the local tenantry was amply testified in a series of public expressions of thanks, in the year before his death. In July 1863, Wilmot was feted at a public dinner with the 'high esteem and appreciation' of his 'public and private worth', not only as a magistrate (having been appointed to the judicial bench for Cheshire and Derbyshire) but as 'a patron of agricultural art'. In response, Wilmot delivered a speech which not only drew (by inference) a telling comparison between his employment under the Dukes of Newcastle and Devonshire but made comments which might be regarded as an epitaph upon his career:

> The duties of a steward are always difficult, and I am well aware I have been guilty of many short comings and omissions; I have, however, done my best, and my duties have been comparatively light, owing to the kind confidence of my employer on the one hand, and the cooperation of the tenantry on the other. I have endeavoured to act justly between those two great interests which are identical and whose obligations are equal – that of landlord and tenant. I have had employers whose views I could not carry out, and as a tenant farmer I have had stewards with whom I could not agree. My wish has been so to act amongst you as I should as a tenant wish a steward to act towards myself.

Later in the year, the Sunday school teachers of Burbage gave a celebratory meal in honour of Emma, when she was presented with a silver cup 'in appreciation of her work for the Sunday school and village'. At the beginning of 1864, Wilmot was guest of honour at a dinner at Burbage Public Hall given by the local Lime Company for their employees, their wives and friends. Responding to the toast, Wilmot summed up his pride in the village and expressed his desire to inculcate the notion of 'self help' - lately popularised through the work of Samuel Smiles - amongst them [55].

However, in the midst of all this, Wilmot's increasing ill-health was becoming a matter of concern. Visiting him in May 1864, the Duke of Devonshire noted, 'Mr Wilmot has been & still is I fear very unwell, & I did not stay long'. Having gone to Harrogate (another noted spa town) to recuperate, Wilmot died from an intestinal illness on 25 June 1864: he was 55. Devonshire expressed his regret at the loss of 'a very good agent' and thought it 'a very serious misfortune to his family'. Whilst his death was noted in the Derbyshire and Nottinghamshire press, it was his high standing in the final decade of his life which his obituaries concentrated upon. Wilmot, they concluded, was 'a man of no common order, [possessing] an industry untiring, and perseverance which no difficulties could daunt' [56].

After Wilmot (1864-1898)

One of the more note-worthy expressions of condolence relayed to Emma, after Wilmot's death, came from the celebrated novelist Elizabeth Gaskell, whose acquaintance Emma had made during her time at Hulme Walfield. Mrs Gaskell had stayed with Emma in December 1852, when she noted that the house was 'a large one...and must be very pretty in fine weather', being full of people 'all talking about things that interest me'. Though the strongest bond between the two families appears to have been between Gaskell's daughter Marianne and Fanny Wilmot, she could not help writing to tell Emma:

how very sorry I am for you. One can say nothing more at such a time. I, who have not been tried, can only faintly imagine what must be the depth of your grief – but God knows, and He will comfort you, as you know well dear friend – in a way which makes all human sympathy seem poor and vain. Yet oh! I am so sorry for you - & Emma & Fanny - & the dear affectionate boys! I can hardly fancy a loss that will be more deeply felt, or by a larger number of people. I used to fancy when I was a child, that when I grew older I should understand the sad and mysterious things of this life; but somehow the older I grow the more sadness and the mystery deepen. 'The night is darkest before the dawn', May we see Light in God's Light when that time comes! [57]

On quitting Hulme Walfield, at the end of 1857, Wilmot, Emma and five of the children (Emma, Fanny, Darwin, Reginald and Edmund) had moved back across the Derbyshire border to settle at Burbage-on-the-Wye, in the parish of Hartington. The Wilmots settled at Wye Head House (afterwards known as 'Wyelands') on St John's Road; a large, stone-built property with two large bays, a blue slate roof and stables, about one mile from Buxton. They continued to live well – in 1861, their household included five servants (including a gardener, a groom and a maid) – and they owned land which came to be known as 'Wilmot's Field': this provided the site of a Brass Band contest on the day before Wilmot's death. Wilmot was regarded as 'popular with everyone, due to his courtesy, business ability, fair dealing and hard work'. The family gave annual oyster suppers at Christmas and an annual New Year's Eve Ball in the Buxton Assembly Rooms for up to 200 guests. There were dinners and suppers for estate workers, children's tea parties and rent audit dinners. In Burbage, Wilmot held lantern shows and tea parties in support of the new school rooms, provided ten allotments for local lime-kiln workers and hosted an annual horticultural show. Supported by Emma, 'who was a popular figure in the village' and 'held in some local esteem', the couple provided visits to nearby Poole's Cavern, an annual tea for the local band, cricket matches and Christmas gifts for children.

Wilmot also had a more lasting impact on the village. Before 1860, many of the lime burners, coal miners and farm labourers who resided in the village had been forced to travel ten miles to Hartington for their religious services. After making representations to the Duke of Devonshire, the latter gave the ground for a new church and graveyard together with a donation of £350 (about one-quarter of the estimated costs of the building work). Wilmot himself subscribed £20 to the church fund. The foundation stone of Christ Church, Burbage was laid by the Duke on 29 August 1860 (the silver trowel being presented to the Duke in remembrance of the event). Following the ceremony, the Wilmots entertained the Duke, Bishop Spencer and an assorted party (including Sir Henry Wilmot, Sir Charles and Lady Anderson and the Boyles) to dinner. The church, containing '300 free and un-appropriated sittings', built to the designs of Henry Currey, was consecrated on 1 August 1861. Together with Isaac Norton, Wilmot became one of Burbage's first churchwardens and hosted an annual September Wakes, thereafter, in commemoration of its foundation [58].

Appropriately enough, Wilmot's funeral and burial took place at the church. The funeral, which was attended by 2000 people, was preceded by the shops closing in Buxton at noon and a procession starting from the Assembly Rooms, by way of Wyelands, to the church. The service was conducted by Reverends Weigall and Bosworth. Wilmot's remains were interred in the new graveyard outside, close to the vestry door, the text on the cross above his gravestone recording 'I know that my redeemer liveth' (Job 19:25) with the Apostles' Creed below: 'I believe in the forgiveness of sins / The Resurrection of the Body/ And the life everlasting'. Inside the church, a memorial raised by public subscription 'by the inhabitants of Burbage and others who appreciated his excellence and lament his decease' was placed on the wall adjoining the vestry. This singled out the church, the school and the provision of water and gas to Burbage as evidence of the 'educational, moral and religious advantages' which he had brought to the locality [59].

With Wilmot's death, the close family circle which had been central to Emma's life began to disperse. Woollett became a Lieutenant in the Royal Marines Light Infantry, enrolling at Chatham in June 1865. After succeeding Lieutenant Liardet as instructor of musketry to the Mediterranean Fleet on 30 March 1878, he died at Malta Hospital on 31 July 1879 from epileptic convulsions following a severe attack of delirium tremens. Meanwhile, Darwin Wilmot, who graduated from Brasenose College, Oxford (BA 1868, MA 1871) and took holy orders, became Assistant Master at Rossall School (near Fleetwood in Lancashire) in 1871 and at Marlborough College in 1874. He went on to become Headmaster of Macclesfield Grammar School in the year that he married Louisa Lilla Bickmore, the daughter of the Reverend Charles Bickmore of Highlands, Leamington. The marriage (which was conducted by the bride's father) took place at All Saints' Church, Leamington, on 3 October 1876 [60]. The family also entrenched its place in Derbyshire county society through the marriage, at

Chaddesden, on 11 October 1866, of Emma Maria Wilmot to Godfrey Franceys Meynell (29 January 1844-18 February 1921). The villagers of Burbage held a celebratory feast in honour of the occasion, the centre piece of which was a bride-cake provided by Emma 'in a pretty rustic basket, in a conspicuous part of the tea-table'. However, Wilmot's absence was not forgotten. As the newspaper report of the festivities observed: 'We have only to add that, in the adjoining church-yard, the quiet grave of one to whom this marriage-day would have been a happy one, was not forgotten, but had been beautifully re-decorated with fresh flowers tastefully arranged in wreaths and festoons' **[61]**.

[Left: Emma and Wilmot's grave in Burbage Churchyard]

Emma's sketchbooks

Emma was only 44 years old when Wilmot died and outlived him by another thirty four years; she died on 22 December 1898 at the age of 78. The intervening years left little public record of her life, except for the periodic appearance of her name amongst the list of relatives and friends who attended the usual round of family events; Emma's thoughtful gifts of Crown Derby porcelain were invariably numbered amongst the wedding presents received by her newly-married relatives. In 1871, Emma was listed as a patroness for a Grand Children's Concert, held at the Drill Hall in Derby. By the time her son Woollett died (in 1879), she was living with her unmarried daughter Fanny and two servants at 173 Ashbourne Road, Derby; by 1881, they had moved to 67 Friar Gate, Derby **[62]**.

At her death, Emma's body was transferred by train from Derby to Buxton; from there she was taken to Burbage Churchyard, where she was laid to rest alongside Wilmot in the graveyard of Christ Church. A simple addition to the grave's headstone recorded the presence of 'Emma Elizabeth, wife of Edward Woollett Wilmot. At Rest'. A wreath of ivy and Christmas roses was placed at the memorial which the people of Burbage had raised to Wilmot inside the church. Later, a brass memorial plaque, in Emma's memory, commissioned by her four surviving children (Emma, Frances, Darwin and Reginald), was placed alongside Wilmot's memorial. The text on it replicated the theme of 'rest' on the couple's headstone: 'Then are they Glad because they are at rest / And so He bringeth them unto the haven / Where they would be' (Psalms, 107:30).

As the grand-daughter of Erasmus Darwin, the cousin of Charles Darwin and the wife of Edward Woollett Wilmot, Emma's life might only have been remembered through her relationship to the eminent male relations in her life were it not for two books of sketches and drawings, relating to her life in Nottinghamshire (many of them annotated as to location, date or subject matter), which descended through the family line. Together, these sketchbooks provide a visual memoir of Emma's early married life, illustrating her impressions of the county in which she and Wilmot probably expected to reside for many years thereafter. In spite of some difference between the two books, in terms of the quality of the illustrations, the contents of both are remarkably fine, recording Emma Wilmot's life and interests as a newly-married woman in the 1840s.

[Right: Memorial plaque to Emma in Burbage Parish Church]

Whilst the larger part of the drawings relate to Nottinghamshire, they also illustrate selective scenes from across Derbyshire, Staffordshire, Shropshire and Yorkshire, focusing upon sites of architectural or picturesque interest and places which held a strong personal meaning for Emma herself. Of the non-Nottinghamshire material (not included here), there are views of Morley Church (close to Breadsall), Sydnope Hall at Darley Dale (her father's property, which was later sold on behalf of the family by Wilmot and her brother Edward), Darley Dale (June 1845), Chaddesden, a Roman Barrow at Skipsea near Bridlington, Park Hall (near Barlborough in Derbyshire) – a property once in the ownership of the Byron family of Newstead - Shrewsbury

(where Charles Darwin's family lived and he was born) and portraits of animals belonging to Sir Henry Wilmot of Chaddesden and Dr Darwin of Shrewsbury **[63]**.

The first (and by far the larger) of the two sketchbooks (containing some 80 pencil sketches, pen and ink drawings and watercolours) was bought by the mother of the present owner for a shilling at an auction in Warwickshire during the 1950s. Given the proximity of Berkswell Hall, the conjectural evidence is that the sketchbook may have passed down the Eardley-Wilmot line - a collateral branch of the Wilmot families of Osmaston and Chaddesden (Derbyshire), whose country residence was Berkswell - before ending up at the sale. During the 1990s, Neville Hoskins, President of Bromley House Subscription Library in Nottingham, had loan of the sketchbook for an extended period and corresponded with the Nottinghamshire agricultural historian Philip Lyth (amongst many others) about its contents. It was as a result of Hoskins' patient detective work that the attribution of the sketches to Emma was achieved (the drawings being generally unsigned). Under the auspices of the Thoroton Society of Nottinghamshire, Hoskins organised coach-parties which went 'in Emma's footsteps', visiting sites to be found in the sketchbook, and lectured to various local history and archaeological societies on the artist's life and times [64].

[Left: Emma's drawing of a waterfall at Sydnope]

During the course of Hoskins' work, a second, finely-tooled sketchbook, bound in leather, with the contents interleaved with tissue, came to light at Bassetlaw Museum in Retford. It was immediately apparent that the drawings (most of which come from c.1846) were by the same artist, for it contained the only drawings to be signed with the initials 'E.E.W'. The book had all the appearance of a 'best' or fine-quality portfolio, which may have been used by Emma for finished drawings of some of the sites featured in her 'rough' or working-out sketchbook (most of which date from c.1842-5). Although a number of images featured in the Retford book do not have corresponding versions in the original sketchbook, all 14 scenes within it relate exclusively to Nottinghamshire. There is no information as to the book's provenance except for a note that it was purchased from the George Gregory Book Store in Bath in October 1959 for £4. This would reinforce the probability that the books had been in common ownership until they were sold (and separated) during the late-1950s. The Retford book was given a new leather spine and repairs were made to its front boards by Cedric Chivers Limited in April 1960 for the sum of £2 and 10 shillings [65].

The practice for young women 'of quality' to keep a sketchbook or engage in the past-time of line drawing and watercolours has long been recognised as one of the 'polite accomplishments' expected of young women with education, interests and breeding during this period; its more distinguished exponents include Lady Charlotte Canning and Queen Victoria [66]. Whilst most of these compositions were designed for a private or family audience (if not solely for the satisfaction of the artist herself), the technical skill and accuracy of detail revealed in drawings of this nature showed that many of the artists had received a degree of training which belied the notion of their 'amateur' or dilettante status.

Armed with her sketching materials and riding out in her gig or pony-cart **[see right]**, Emma's drawings represent a visual journal illustrating her impressions and experiences of Nottinghamshire life in the 1840s. Whether she continued this habit after leaving the county is not known, as no further sketchbooks have come to light.

Wilmot and Emma undoubtedly lived the life of a strongly committed married couple, actuated by a sense of family, faith and community; they were resolutely 'Victorian' in combining a belief in self-help with a concern for the material improvement of those less fortunate than themselves. This actuated Wilmot professionally and was lived out, with Emma, through acts of kindness and generosity towards the families of tenants and estate workers; more especially, in the latter part of their life, when they had the security of permanent employment and a strong reservoir of support in the community where they lived. It is not coincidental that they were the friends of Elizabeth Gaskell, whose novels portrayed lives of community involvement and reciprocity between the social classes yet whose characters were often only a whisker away from financial or social ruin. In bringing Emma's

sketchbooks of Nottinghamshire life in the 1840s in to public view, we not only discover an artist of some considerable merit but recover a way of life which textual sources, by themselves, can seldom portray.

[Emma Wilmot with her pony and cart]

REFERENCES

[1] University of Nottingham Manuscripts and Special Collections [UNMASC], Ne C 8717/2, Wilmot to Newcastle, 30 December 1841.

[2] *Morning Post*, 18 November 1836.

[3] *Derby Mercury*, 2 December 1896; *Morning Post*, 2 December 1896. The funeral service was conducted by Reverend F.E.W. Wilmot (Edmund's cousin); as Vicar of Burbage, Wilmot conducted Emma's funeral service, two years later.

[4] *Derby Mercury*, 15 March 1854. Lucy Helen Muriel Soulsby became a headmistress and noted author of devotional and educational books: Kate Flint, 'Lucy Helen Muriel Soulsby', *The Oxford Dictionary of National Biography* (online edition, 2004-2012).

[5] See *Derby Mercury*, 18, 25 September 1839, regarding the sale of this livestock on 4 October 1839,

[6] *Derby Mercury*, 19 September 1832, 4 October 1837; UNMASC, Ne C 7819/1, Wilmot to Newcastle, 3 December 1839; *Preston Chronicle*, 8 February 1840.

[7] Nottinghamshire Archives, DD/1440/103. The map is also significant because it reproduces Wilmot's coat of arms.

[8] Newcastle Diary, 12 March, 10 August 1838: Richard A Gaunt, (editor), *Unhappy Reactionary: The Diaries of the Fourth Duke of Newcastle-under-Lyne*, 1822-50 (Thoroton Society Record Series, Nottingham, 2003), p.217.

[9] UNMASC, Ne C 7766, Wilmot to Newcastle, *circa* 15 December 1838 (dated from enclosed letter at Ne C 7767). Wilmot ceased his employment with Scarbrough, after two years as his agent, in 1838. For Wilmot's later dealings with Scarbrough, see UNMASC, NW 236, Wilmot to Newcastle (undated, *circa* 1840), referring to the Wellow enclosure.

[10] Newcastle Diary, 16 November 1838: *Unhappy Reactionary*, p.220; UNMASC, Ne C 8432, John Beasley to Newcastle, 18 August 1838.

[11] Newcastle Diary, 25 June 1847: *Unhappy Reactionary*, pp.270-71; UNMASC, Ne C 7806, Wilmot to Newcastle, 30 September 1839; Mellor & Beer Estate Agents, Worksop, sales particulars (2012). Wilmot made alterations to Sparken House, at his own expense, which (he assured the Duke) did not alter its external appearance: UNMASC, NW 235/1, Wilmot to Newcastle, 19 September 1840. For the late-nineteenth century history of the property, see UNMASC, Ne D 4385 and Hull History Centre, U/DX/103/18.

[12] UNMASC, Ne C 7766, dated *circa* 15 December 1838; *England & Wales, FreeBMD Death Index*: 1837-1915, XV, 407 registers the death of Augusta Matilda Wilmot in October-December 1838. In the 1841 Census, Wilmot's household comprised himself and three children under ten (Lucy, Robert and Edmund): The National Archives, Kew (TNA), HO/107/852.

[13] UNMASC, Ne C 7819, Wilmot to Newcastle, 3 December 1839; Ne C 7871, Wilmot to Newcastle, 7 June 1845; Ne C 7966, Wilmot to Newcastle, 28 May 1847.

[14] UNMASC, Ne C 7897, Wilmot to Newcastle, 16 February 1846; Ne C 7898, Wilmot to Newcastle, 23 January 1846; Ne C 7965, Wilmot to Newcastle, 27 May 1847.

[15] UNMASC, Ne C 7858/1-2, Wilmot to Newcastle, August 1844; Ne C 7930, Wilmot to Newcastle, 1 April 1847; Ne C 7937, John Wilson to Wilmot, 29 March 1847.

[16] UNMASC, Ne C 7867/1-2, Wilmot to Newcastle, 18 February 1845.

[17] UNMASC, Ne C 7814, Wilmot to Newcastle, 17 November 1839; cf. Ne C 7950, Wilmot to Newcastle, 28 April 1847.

[18] UNMASC, Ne C 7815/1, undated, Wilmot to Newcastle; Ne C 7842/1-3, Wilmot to Newcastle, 18 June 1843; Ne C 7844/1-2, *circa* June 1843; Newcastle Diary, 29 May 1843: *Unhappy Reactionary*, p.242.

[19] UNMASC, Ne C 7849/1, Wilmot to Newcastle, 20 May 1844; Ne C 7858/1-2, Wilmot to Newcastle, *circa* 23-27 August 1844; Ne C 7897, Wilmot to Newcastle, 16 February 1846; Newcastle Diary, 13 March 1847: *Unhappy Reactionary*, p.268.

[20] UNMASC, Ne C 6854, Parkinson to Newcastle, 10 June 1839.

[21] East Sussex Record Office, FRE/2935, Wilmot to Frewen, 30 October 1844; FRE/2945, Wilmot to Frewen, 12 October 1850.

[22] *The Standard*, 9 May 1845; UNMASC, Ne C 8259, Wilmot to Newcastle, 7 May 1845; cf. Ne C 7943, Wilmot to Newcastle, 16 April 1847.

[23] *Morning Post*, 6 November 1845; UNMASC, Ne C 7917, Wilmot to Newcastle, 4 July 1846.

[24] UNMASC, Ne C 7953, Wilmot to Newcastle, 2 May 1847; cf. Ne C 7950, Wilmot to Newcastle, 28 April 1847. Wilmot regularly valued land which was purchased by railway companies for their lines: House of Commons Parliamentary Papers (HOC [PP]), 1849 (574), *Second report of the Select Committee on the Woods, Forests, and Land Revenues of the Crown; together with the minutes of evidence, appendix, and index*, Appendix F.

[25] Newcastle Diary, 16, 25 June 1841: *Unhappy Reactionary*, pp.128-29.

[26] See Richard A Gaunt, 'Keeping it in the Family: political patronage in early nineteenth century Nottinghamshire', *Transactions of the Thoroton Society of Nottinghamshire*, 115 (2011), 159-80.

[27] *Morning Post*, 27 January 1844; UNMASC, Ne C 4575, Wilmot to Lincoln, 28 December 1845.

[28] UNMASC, Ne C 4606, Wilmot to Lincoln, 4 February 1846; Ne C 4608, Wilmot to Lincoln, 6 February 1846, for Wilmot's detailed election and canvassing advice. Amongst other things, Wilmot thought Godfrey Tallents was a 'wet blanket'; cf. *Unhappy Reactionary*, pp.144-45.

[29] UNMASC, Ne C 4578, Wilmot to Lincoln, 2 January 1846; Ne C 4579/1-2, Godfrey Tallents to Lincoln, 2 January 1846; *Morning Post*, 2 January 1846.

[30] The Nottingham Estates of the Dukes of Newcastle had been removed from the Clumber Collection in 1821 to constitute a separate collection comprising estates at Nottingham, Basford, Brinsley, Calverton, Cropwell Butler, Flawborough and Hucknall. The Clumber Collection included Beckingham, Bevercotes, Bothamsall, Cromwell, West Drayton, Elkesley, Egmanton, Eaton, Gamston, Haughton, Haughton Park, Holme and Muskham, Kirton, Lound Hall, Lowdham, Mansfield, Morton, Marnham, East and West Markham, Milton and Tuxford, Martin and Scaftworth, Mattersey, Maplebeck, Ordsall, Ollerton, Stockwith [West], Walesby, Wheatley and Walkeringham and Misterton.

[31] UNMASC, Ne C 7898, Wilmot to Newcastle, 23 January 1846. Wilmot had first become familiar with Nottingham in 1827: HOC [PP], 1847-48 (461), *Report from the Select Committee on Agricultural Customs; together with the minutes of evidence, and index*, p.58.

[32] UNMASC, Ne C 7897, Wilmot to Newcastle, 16 February 1846; Ne C 4625, Wilmot to Lincoln, 20 February 1846.

[33] UNMASC, Ne C 4636, Wilmot to Lincoln, 16 March 1846.

[34] UNMASC, Ne C 4644, Wilmot to Lincoln, 23 May 1846; Ne C 7986, Wilmot to Newcastle, 4 July 1847.

[35] UNMASC, Hn R 1/14; Hn R 1/15/1-8.

[36] TNA, IR 29/5/52; 29/5/92; 29/5/258; 30/5/258; 29/5/356; 30/5/356; 29/8/45; 30/8/35; UNMASC, Ne C 4636, Wilmot to Lincoln, 16 March 1846; *Derby Mercury*, 23 May 1849.

[37] UNMASC, Ne C 7983, Wilmot to Newcastle, 17 June 1847.

[38] Newcastle Diary, 20 November 1847: *Unhappy Reactionary*, p.273.

[39] UNMASC, Ne C 7975, Wilmot to Newcastle, 8 June 1847; Ne C 7986, Wilmot to Newcastle, 4 July 1847.

[40] UNMASC, Ne C 7997/1-2, Heming to Newcastle, 3 August 1847.

[41] UNMASC, Ne C 8003, Wilmot to Newcastle, 24 August 1847.

[42] Newcastle Diary, 25 June 1847: *Unhappy Reactionary*, pp.270-71.

[43] UNMASC, Ne C 8016, Wilmot to Newcastle, 6 November 1847; Ne C 6524, Smith & Company to Newcastle, 11 June 1849.

[44] UNMASC, Ne C 6485/1-2, Newcastle to Wilmot, 8 April 1849.

[45] UNMASC, Ne C 6486, Wilmot to Newcastle, 10 April 1849; cf. Ne C 8086/1-4, Heming to Newcastle, 28 July 1849, which quotes extensively from a letter from Wilmot to Heming.

[46] UNMASC, Ne C 8085/1-2, Heming to Newcastle, 22 July 1849; Ne C 8086/1-4, Heming to Newcastle, 28 July 1849; also see note 18 above. In spite of their differences, Wilmot attended the 4th Duke's funeral in January 1851: Michael B Chambers, *The Fourth Duke of Newcastle* (n.y.), p.23.

[47] UNMASC, Ne C 8013/1-3, Heming to Newcastle, 19 October 1847; Ne C 4644, Wilmot to Lincoln, 23 May 1846; *Derby Mercury*, 23 June 1847. By his own admission, Wilmot was farming 100 acres and acting as the agent for several large properties in Nottinghamshire, Derbyshire, Leicestershire, Lancashire and Cheshire by March 1848: *Select Committee on Agricultural Customs*, p.55.

[48] *The Standard*, 6 July 1848; for the history of the area, see Earl Cyrus Warburton, *The Warburtons of Warburton and Arley* (1956).

[49] 1851 Census: TNA, HO 107/2167.

[50] Cork City and County Archives, SM620, Midleton Estate Report (1850); *Select Committee on Agricultural Customs*, pp. 15, 55-68; *Daily News*, 8 November 1850; George Wingrove Cooke, *A treatise on the law of agricultural tenancies; with forms and precedents* (1850), pp.381-84.

[51] *The Morning Chronicle*, 20 September 1848; *Blackburn Standard*, 28 July 1852.

[52] *Derby Mercury*, 4 February 1857.

[53] *Sheffield and Rotherham Independent*, 20 September 1856; *Derby Mercury*, 4 September 1861; HOC [PP], 1862 [2930] [2932] [2935] [2938] [2980], *Turnpike trusts. England and Wales. General report, made by direction of the Secretary of State under act 3 & 4 Wm. IV. Cap. 80*, pp.16-17; Chatsworth House Archives, 7th Duke of Devonshire's Diary, Volume 15, p.130, 4 December 1862. For details of Wilmot's time as agent at Buxton, I am indebted to E M Barton, *Edward Woollett Wilmot 1809*[sic]*-1864. Duke of Devonshire's Agent in Buxton 1856-1864* (unpublished typescript, August 1994).

[54] Chatsworth House Archives, 7th Duke's Diary, Volume 16, p.81, 25 November 1863; for Devonshire's relations with Wilmot during his agency, see Volume 13, pp.53-4, 11-12 April 1859; Volume 15, p.85, 4 August 1862; ibid., p.171, 6 April 1863; Volume 16, p.107, 20 February 1864; ibid., p.114, 1 April 1864.

[55] *Derby Mercury*, 8 July 1863; Barton, *Wilmot*; Samuel Smiles, *Self-Help* (1859) was published in the same year as Darwin's *Origin of Species*. Wilmot was first appointed to the magistrate's bench for Congleton, Cheshire on 4 May 1852: HOC [PP], 1859 Session 2 (2) (96) *Justices of the Peace. Return of the several boroughs and of the several counties of cities and towns in England and Wales... for which persons have been assigned to act as justices of the peace...*, p.3.

[56] Chatsworth House Archives, 7th Duke's Diary, Volume 16, p.132, 19 May 1864; ibid., pp.154-55, 29 June 1864; *Derby Mercury*, 29 June, 6 July 1864; *Nottinghamshire Guardian*, 1 July 1864; *Sheffield and Rotherham Independent*, 2 July 1864. Wilmot's estate was valued under £4,000 when probate was granted on 22 September 1864: England and Wales, National Probate Calendar (Index of Wills & Administrations), 1861-1941 (online database).

[57] J A V Chapple and Arthur Pollard, (editors), *The Letters of Mrs Gaskell* (Manchester, 1966), pp.216-17; cf. 591, 690, 816, 915, 917-18; John Chapple and Alan Shelston, *Further Letters of Mrs Gaskell* (Manchester, 2004), pp.79, 180, 264.

[58] Chatsworth House Archives, 7th Duke's Diary, Volume 14, pp.30-31, 29 August 1860; Barton, *Wilmot*; 1861 Census: TNA, RG/9/2545; [Anon.] *Christ Church Burbage. A Look at the Church and a Brief History* (n.y.).

[59] A mural monument, raised by public subscription, 'in grateful recognition of [Wilmot's] energy and judgement in promoting the interests of the Town and neighbourhood of Buxton', was also placed at the Parish Church of St John the Baptist, Buxton: Cicely M Williams, *The Parish Church of St John the Baptist, Buxton. A Short History and Guide* (n.y.), pp.5-6; Derbyshire Record Office, D6710/1/2/1; D6710/1/1/30.

[60] For Wollett: *Derby Mercury*, 14 April 1847, 13 August 1879; *Morning Post*, 8 July 1865; *Hampshire Advertiser*, 24 April 1878; TNA, ADM/196/61. Woollett left an estate valued under £200 when probate was granted on 16 October 1879: England and Wales, National Probate Calendar (Index of Wills & Administrations), 1861-1941 (online database). For Darwin: *Derby Mercury*, 11 October 1876; *Oxford University Alumni*, 1500-1886, IV (1715-1886), 1579 (online database); T W Ashworth, (editor), *The Rossall Register, 1844-1894* (1895), p.61. Darwin Wilmot published *A Short History of the Grammar School Macclesfield, 1503-1910* (1910), in the year that he retired as Headmaster, and possessed many manuscripts relating to the lives of Erasmus and Francis Sacheverel Darwin: Karl Pearson, *The Life, Letters and Labours of Francis Galton*, Volume 1 (Cambridge, 1914), p.viii.

[61] *Derby Mercury*, 17 October 1866; *Nottinghamshire Guardian*, 19 October 1866. Of Emma's other children, Reginald Mead Wilmot married Melinda Daniel of Burford, Ontario (Canada), on 14 March 1893.

[62] *Derby Mercury*, 29 November 1871, 18 June 1873, 8 January 1890, 20 September 1893, 24 October 1894, 28 April 1897; England and Wales, National Probate Calendar (Index of Wills & Administrations), 1861-1941 (online database); 1871 Census: TNA, RG/10/3569; 1881 Census: TNA, RG/11/3398; Fanny continued to act as the faithful companion of family and friends; for her friendship with Bessie Wheler (the sister of Charles Darwin's cousin Francis Galton), see Karl Pearson, *The Life, Letters and Labours of Francis Galton*, Volume 3b (Cambridge, 1930), pp.548, 552.

[63] *Derby Mercury*, 9 July 1851, for the sale notice of the Sydnope estate; in the event, the property remained in the family's possession until 1858.

[64] Robin Fryer to the author, 7 June 2011; UNMASC, MS 823/4/6/1-2, Neville Hoskins to Philip Lyth, 14, 29 July 1994; Hoskins' research materials on Emma Wilmot (in the author's possession).

[65] Bassetlaw Museum, Retford, Reference 26.86.

[66] Delia Millar, *Watercolours by Charlotte, Viscountess Canning* (Harewood House, 1996); Marina Warner, *Queen Victoria's Sketchbook* (1979).

AGRICULTURAL LIFE

Though Wilmot came to play an important part in the urban development of Buxton, the majority of his professional life and interests were bound up with the countryside and with the promotion and development of agriculture. It is unsurprising, therefore, that Emma should have taken a keen interest in the livestock and farming practices upon which agriculture still relied during the 1840s, before the intensive practices of 'High Farming' came to dominate thinking amongst landowners and farmers. Wilmot's success as a breeder of livestock (sheep, pigs, cattle, oxen, poultry and horses) has already been noted; here, attention may be drawn to Emma's expertise in representing animals (especially horses) in a skilful and believable fashion. Many of the scenes in Emma's sketchbooks have an overwhelmingly rural dimension to them and many feature animals, sometimes as a pleasing foreground designed to alleviate a sense of open, unrelieved space, more usually as the central feature of the illustrations themselves.

The importance of animal husbandry was always appreciated by Wilmot, who became a successful and much sought-after judge of livestock at agricultural shows. On 21 October 1841, Wilmot became Honorary Secretary and Treasurer of the newly-formed Worksop Labourers Friend Society (under the Presidency of the Duke of Newcastle) which was designed to promote the material welfare of agricultural labourers and promote effective agricultural practices

amongst them [1]. Wilmot's concern for the proper care and breeding of livestock also emerges from a letter he wrote to the Duke on 13 April 1845, following the theft of some sheep from one of Newcastle's tenant farms: 'the duty of a shepherd is to count his sheep twice a day - without doing this, things cannot go on well - when I kept sheep, had my man not done so, and I detected him, I should have dismissed him at once - I merely name this, to shew [*sic*] how strongly I feel the duty of a shepherd - who has more responsibility than almost any other servant on a large farm' [2].

[1] *The Hull Packet*, 15 October 1841.

[2] UNMASC, Ne C 7473.

ILLUSTRATIONS

Deer Park Worksop Manor
1842

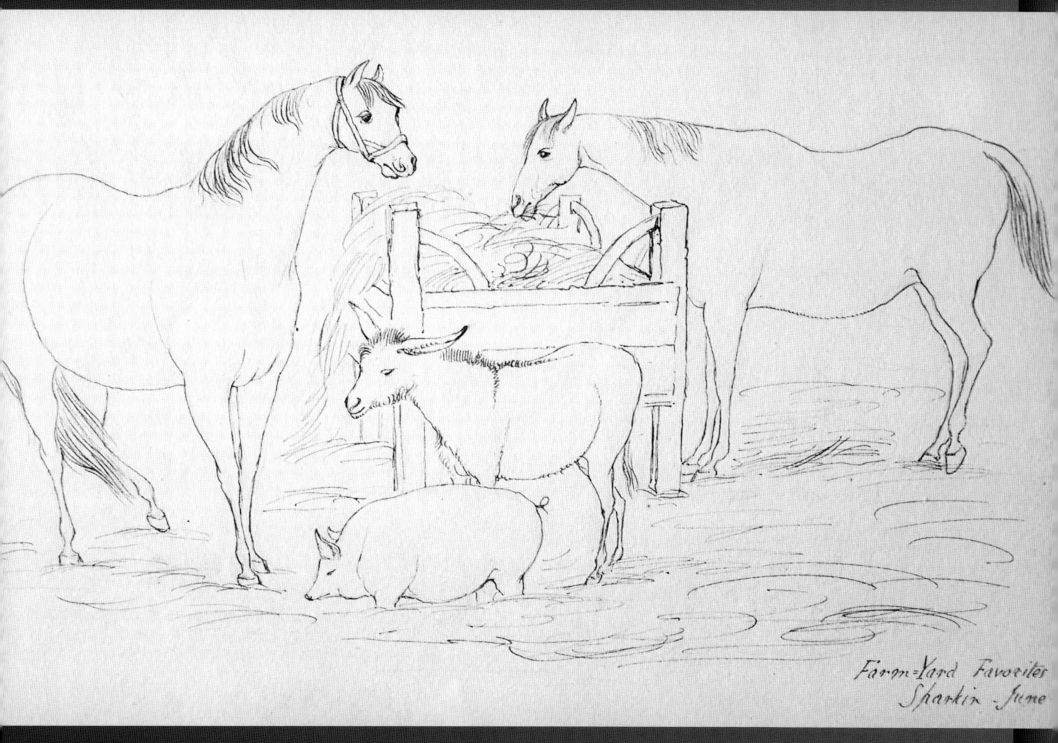

Farm=Yard Favorites
Sharkin June

COUNTRY ESTATES

In 1856, on visiting north Nottinghamshire, the future 7th Duke of Devonshire noted his impressions of 'Shirewood [sic] Forest':

> The old forest is most striking & I did not expect to see such numbers of fine old oaks still standing. The one part called Birkland there are numbers of fine birches mixed with the oaks. The whole is covered thickly with bracken. Both Thoresby & Clumber are built on too low ground, but Clumber has a fine artificial lake in front & an Italian garden [1].

Devonshire's interest in the landscape which Emma and Wilmot knew from their time in the county reveals its continuing hold upon the imagination of visitors, of whatever rank and station. Long known as 'the most aristocratic of counties' because of the nature and density of its landed estates, the historic realm of the Nottinghamshire 'Dukeries' (Newcastle of Clumber, Portland of Welbeck, Kingston of Thoresby and Norfolk of Worksop) was, nevertheless, undergoing a period of transformation. Not only were these estates subject to the usual vicissitudes of spendthrift aristocrats, family rivalries, economic pressures and problems of inheritance and succession, but the shape and nature of the landscape of country estates was undergoing modification. Landscape designers such as William Gilpin, working to the fashionable principles of 'picturesque' design (after the manner of works of art), were transforming Clumber during the period [2],

whilst Colonel Thomas Wildman's ownership of the Newstead Abbey estate saw major structural work in an attempt to preserve and augment its historic fabric; this included the relocation of the ancient font (or fountain) to the cloisters. Other locations, still extant in Emma's day, such as Blyth Hall (the seat of the Mellish family), no longer exist: the Hall was demolished in 1972. When one encompasses estates on the borders of Nottinghamshire, such as ancient Hardwick Hall ('more glass than wall') and the atmospheric remains of Creswell Crags (a major site of archaeological interest), it is clear that Emma Wilmot did not lack for potential sites of historic interest.

A different sort of atmosphere was leant by the famous oak trees of Welbeck Park. The 'Seven Sisters' Oak was named because it had seven trunks issuing from a single root; it reached a height of about 90 feet. Conversely, the fame of the Greendale Oak was already established by the time that John Evelyn featured it in his *Sylvia* (1670). Its subsequent celebrity was established when, in 1725, Lord Harley, 2nd Earl of Oxford, who succeeded to the Welbeck estate through his wife, 'declared that he had a tree in his park with a sufficiently large trunk to allow an aperture to be cut, through which a coach and six could be driven' [3]. Thus, by the time that Emma Wilmot represented it in her sketchbook, the Greendale (or 'Grindall') Oak had been forming an arborial road-way for well over a century.

[1] Chatsworth House Archives, 7th Duke of Devonshire's Diary, Volume 11, pp.81-82, 23 January 1856.

[2] Richard A Gaunt, 'Crafting Clumber. The Dukes of Newcastle and the Nottinghamshire Landscape', *Landscape History*, 33:1 (2012), 87-102, examines this process and reproduces two of Emma's drawings of Clumber from the Retford sketchbook.

[3] J Rodgers, *The Scenery of Sherwood Forest with an Account of Some Eminent People Once Resident There* (1908), pp.292-93, quoted in Charles Watkins, (editor), *European Woods and Forests. Studies in Cultural History* (1998), pp.101-03.

ILLUSTRATIONS

Clumber
1842

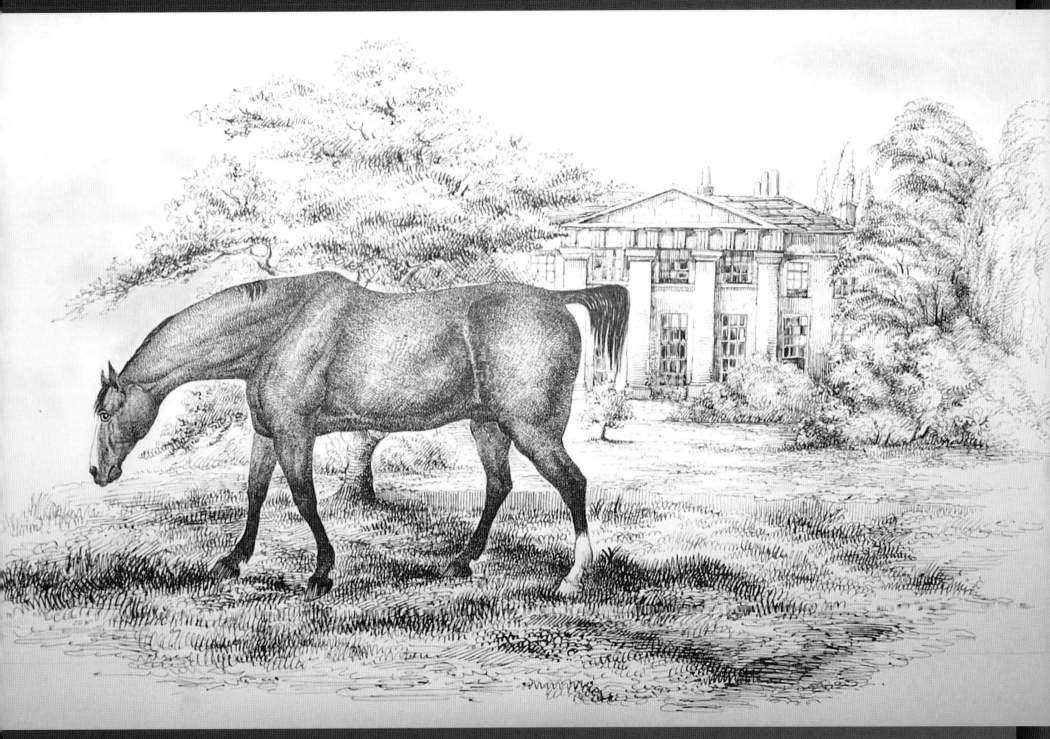

Blyth

WORKSOP SCENES

Emma's arrival in Worksop, in January 1842, coincided with important changes in the historic fabric of the town; changes which she was uniquely placed to observe and illustrate. The Priory Church of Our Lady and St Cuthbert (formerly the site of a 12th Century Augustinian monastery) underwent a major restoration programme between 1845 and 1849 by Nicholson of Lincoln. This resulted in the re-roofing and re-slating of the church, new foundations for the south tower and the restoration of the pillars and south aisle to a vertical position. In addition, 'the Tudor window in the eastern blocking was replaced by one of three lights, three decorated windows were removed from the south aisle and both aisles were restored with pseudo-Norman windows, the glazing removed from the triforium, as pitched; roofs now covered the aisles, the whole was re-paved and re-seated' [1]. Emma contributed to this restoration with a donation of £100, half of which was allocated for the alteration work, half to the provision of furniture and pew cushions for the pulpit and reading desk and for a new altar cloth. Though she left Worksop before the restoration work was complete, Emma made good her promise by despatching, from Congleton, a new altar cloth for the church. This was made from:

costly crimson silk velvet, embroidered with yellow silk needlework. The figures are alternately crimson and yellow. The borders, which are yellow, represent the *fleur de lis*. In the centre of the valance for the pulpit, the characters of "I.H.S.", in ancient church text, are inlaid in yellow needlework, surrounding which is a border of the same material and colour. The valance for the reading desk is considerably shorter, but very beautiful. In the centre of the front of the altar covering, the corresponding characters, "I.H.S.", also appear, and are encircled with a rich ornamental yellow device. The carpet of the altar steps is figured to match [2].

Equally significant was the dismantling of the incomplete Palladian manor house at Worksop. This had been designed by James Paine as a replacement for the former house, which had been consumed by fire in 1761. Only a single wing (of 23 bays) had been completed for the 9th Duke of Norfolk by 1767 and the project had gone into abeyance thereafter. However, following the purchase of the Worksop Manor estate by the 4th Duke of Newcastle in 1838-9, the house was dismantled during the period 1842-6. Emma's illustrations constitute a unique record of that process.

[1] Colin Walker, *The Priory Church of Our Lady and St Cuthbert, Worksop, Notts* (7th edition, 1975), pp.18-19.

[2] *The Morning Post*, 22 July 1850; regrettably, none of these items is extant.

ILLUSTRATIONS

Worksop Church

OTHER FEATURED PICTURES

Front Cover: Starting for the show at Retford (Sparken, 1 October 1842).

Inside Front Cover: Sparken Hill, Worksop.

Page 06: Two of Emma's step-children.

Page 08: Emma and Wilmot, at the entrance to Steetley Chapel.

Page 34: Unidentified figures (possibly including Emma and Wilmot on the right).

Page 77: Emma, Wilmot and their friends.

Inside Back Cover: Oaks near Welbeck.

Back Cover: Creswell Crags.

ACKNOWLEDGEMENTS

My principal acknowledgement must be to Robin Fryer, the owner of the first and fullest of Emma Wilmot's sketchbooks, for granting me permission to reproduce illustrations from it and for providing information about the book's likely provenance. I am also grateful to Bassetlaw Museum, Retford, the custodian of the other sketchbook, for similar permission to publish. Mark Dorrington was a supportive advocate of the project from its inception and I express my gratitude to Nottinghamshire County Council for once again allowing me to make my research available to a wider audience through the auspices of its publications programme. The University of Nottingham's Manuscripts and Special Collections hold the 4th Duke of Newcastle's diaries and Wilmot's correspondence with Newcastle, the Earl of Lincoln and others, which proved essential to telling the story of the family during the period covered by the sketchbooks. I also express my gratitude to the Trustees, Chatsworth House Settlement (by permission of the Duke of Devonshire), for permission to reproduce material from the Devonshire Collection (7th Duke's series). James Towe, archivist at Chatsworth, is due my particular thanks. A similar debt of gratitude is due to Joyce Allwright, Churchwarden, Christ Church, Burbage, for providing me with documentation relating to the couple's time in the village. I am similarly grateful to Jean Luton, Churchwarden, St John's, Buxton, for facilitating access to the Wilmot memorial in the church. Frank Underwood, Churchwarden, Priory Church of Our Lady and St Cuthbert at Worksop, proved a knowledgeable guide to the church and subsequently uncovered the memorial to Augusta, Wilmot's first wife.

My introduction to Emma and Wilmot arose out of my work on (and abiding interest in) the 4th Duke of Newcastle but it was Neville Hoskins who first drew attention to Emma's sketchbooks and made their contents more widely known. I am particularly indebted to Neville's widow, Ann, who allowed me access to the Fryer sketchbook whilst it was still in her possession, and their son David, who passed on his father's research material to me. Though I have independently sought out and researched the life and times of Emma and Edward Woollett Wilmot, I have always done so in the knowledge that, without the Hoskins, and their friend and coadjutor Rosalys Coope, to whom the larger of the two sketchbooks was first introduced, they might have remained undiscovered. It is thus not only fitting but a genuine pleasure for me to dedicate the book, in grateful remembrance, to Neville Hoskins – I hope he would have enjoyed it.